Which Bib[le]
Version:

NKJV | RSV
NIV | ASV | NASB
RSV | CEV | TNIV | AV
B | AV | NLT | REB | A

say unto him, Master, this woman was taken in adultery, in the very act.
Moses in the law commanded us, that such should be stoned: but what sayest thou
said, tempting him, that they might have to accuse him. But Jesus stooped do
continued asking him, he lifted up himself, and said unto them, He that is
heard it, being co... on the ... ground
lifted up himself, and saw ... science went out one by
And Jesus said unto her, Neither do I condemn
unto them, saying, I am the light of the w...

Does it Really Matter?

David Blunt

Which Bible Version: Does it Really Matter?

Product Code: A121

ISBN 978 1 86228 314 5

© 2007 Trinitarian Bible Society
William Tyndale House, 29 Deer Park Road
London SW19 3NN, England

Registered Charity Number: 233082 (England) SC038379 (Scotland)
Copyright is held by the Incorporated Trinitarian Bible Society Trust
on behalf of the Trinitarian Bible Society.

www.tbsbibles.org

10M/09/19

Which Bible Version:
Does it Really Matter?

(Based on an address given by the Rev. David Blunt to
the TBS Day Conference held in Inverness, Scotland, October 2003)

The subject of Bible versions is by no means an academic one, as some may think. It may have academic aspects to it but it is really a very personal subject which affects every believer. We trust that we have all been called by the grace of God to know and love the Lord Jesus Christ. Our desire now is to glorify and to enjoy God. We believe that the Word of God is the only rule to direct us in this our chief end and we believe that the Word of God is to be found only in the Bible. If we are to glorify and enjoy God then we are bound to make use of the Bible. But **which** Bible are we to use? There are a great many versions on offer today. We must therefore make a choice of one version from among the many. Which one will it be? Will it be the Authorised Version? Will it be a modern version? Does it really matter? Every Christian should have a keen interest in this subject.

■ Satan's Strategy

Before answering the specific question, 'Which Version: Does it Really Matter?' we need to establish a very important point. The fact is often overlooked that there is someone else who is interested in our subject. The devil has a very keen interest indeed in the Scriptures. That should not surprise us when we understand that the Word is the chief means whereby God makes Himself known. The Psalmist said, '…thou hast magnified thy word above all thy name' (Psalm 138.2). Satan does not wish God to be known—at least not **in a saving way**. The devil's interest in the Word of God is therefore a malicious one. We ignore this fact at our peril.

The Bible itself shows us Satan's strategy concerning Scripture. We may see it in connection with the very first words which God spoke to man: 'Of every tree of the garden thou mayest freely eat: but of the tree of the knowledge of good and evil, thou shalt not eat of it: for in the day that thou eatest thereof thou shalt surely die' (Genesis 2.16–17).

That was the **original** text. What did Satan do with it? He **queried** it. Appearing as a serpent he said to the woman, 'Yea, hath God said, Ye shall not eat of every tree of the garden?' (Genesis 3.1). Satan's strategy is in various ways to sow doubt in our minds concerning the Word of God.

What was the result of Satan's strategy? We see it in the woman's response to the serpent. 'We may eat of the fruit of the trees of the garden: but of the fruit of the tree which *is* in the midst of the garden, God hath said, Ye shall not eat of it, neither shall ye touch it, lest ye die' (Genesis 3.2–3).

That was the **new** text. The original text which God had given was altered. Three things happened:

Omission: Eve **omitted** the words 'every' ('every tree') and 'freely' ('freely eat').
Addition: Eve **added** the words 'neither shall ye touch it'.
Substitution: Eve **substituted** the words 'lest ye die' for 'thou shalt surely die'.

Thus was born the first 'revised version' of the Word of God. It is the paradigm for Satan's attempts down through history to nullify the Word of God.

This strategy was seen when the Lord Jesus Christ appeared in this world. When he tempted Christ in the wilderness the devil was so bold as to quote the Scriptures to the Son of God. Luke has the fullest account of this incident. This is how he describes the third and final temptation:

And he brought him to Jerusalem, and set him on a pinnacle of the temple, and said unto him, If thou be the Son of God, cast thyself down from hence: for it is written, He shall give his angels charge over thee, to keep thee: and in *their* hands they shall bear thee up, lest at any time thou dash thy foot against a stone. (Luke 4.9–11)

Here is a precious promise for God's people: preservation in time of trouble and danger. It is a quote from the Book of Psalms—and yet it is a **misquote**. The original reads:

For he shall give his angels charge over thee, to keep thee in all thy ways.

They shall bear thee up in *their* hands, lest thou dash thy foot against a stone. (Psalm 91.11–12)

The devil omitted the words 'in all thy ways' from the first part of the verse and added the words 'at any time' to the second part and so perverted the meaning of the text. God's promise that He will keep His own is only to be enjoyed within certain limits—as we walk in His ways, in the paths of righteousness. We never have a license to sin and we have no warrant from God for reckless conduct. It is therefore presumption to expect the Lord to keep us if we are bent on folly. Well did Christ respond to Satan with a text from Deuteronomy quoted accurately and in context: 'It is said, Thou shalt not **tempt** the Lord thy God' (Luke 4.12).

Oh, the subtlety of Satan! This is his great hallmark. 'Now the serpent was more **subtil** than any beast of the field which the LORD God had made' (Genesis 3.1). 'But I fear, lest by any means, as the serpent beguiled Eve through his **subtilty**, so your minds should be corrupted from the simplicity that is in Christ' (2 Corinthians 11.3). Yes, the devil is behind the banning of the Bible and the burning of the Bible, but he is also historically behind the **blurring** of the Bible through the circulation of a revised or altered text. Consider that! It has profound implications for our present day when there are competing texts of the Word of God in circulation. The church is confused and the world is bemused. How clever a strategy the devil has employed! You see, if people lose confidence in the inspiration, purity and trustworthiness of the Word of God then the devil has won, no matter that those same people still hold a copy of some version or other of the Bible in their hands—or more likely by then, have a copy somewhere on their shelves, rarely studied or prayed over.

The devil seeks to alter the Word of God. We have noted the three main types of textual change he sponsors: omission, addition, substitution. We may say a little more about each of these. In each instance the words which are affected are highlighted.

1. Omission

Omission of material found in the Authorised Version (AV) is the **main** type of alteration found in the modern versions. The New Testament of one popular modern version, the New International Version (NIV), first published in 1973, omits seventeen complete verses found in the AV—a figure applicable to most modern versions. Among these are Matthew 18.11: 'For the Son of man is come to save that which was lost', and Acts 8.37: 'And Philip said, If thou believest with all thine heart, thou mayest. And he answered and said, I believe that Jesus Christ is the Son of God'.

Even more serious in a sense is the removal of **portions** of verses—the omission of phrases and clauses which make up complete verses. It is more serious because it also affects the meaning but tends to be less noticed by the reader or hearer. The NIV omits nearly two hundred significant portions of verses.

An important example is the conclusion of the Lord's Prayer in Matthew 6.13: 'For thine is the kingdom, and the power, and the glory, for ever. Amen'. What encouragement to pray the disciples must have received when they heard from the lips of their Lord these words of praise and confidence—words that they were to make their own in prayer! And those who use modern versions are robbed of them! To be consistent those who believe the modern versions to be superior should remove the final question and answer from the *Westminster Shorter Catechism*[1] ('What doth the conclusion of the Lord's prayer teach us?')! We wonder why this is not done? Is it because inwardly they know that this clause is genuine and they tremble at the warnings in Scripture not to take away words from the Word of God (Revelation 22.19)?

Another omission is found in:

◾ Mark 10.24
AV: Children, how hard is it **for them that trust in riches** to enter into the kingdom of God!
NIV: Children, how hard it is to enter the kingdom of God!

The NIV in the previous verse has Jesus saying to the disciples, 'How hard it is for the rich to enter the kingdom of God!' The NIV presents the truth, but not the **whole** truth. It is not wealth itself which is an obstacle to entering God's kingdom, but the fact that people tend to put their **trust** in their wealth rather than in God. 'Lo, *this is* the man *that* made not God his strength; but trusted in the abundance of his riches, *and* strengthened himself in his wickedness' (Psalm 52.7). That was the rich young ruler's problem. Though Matthew and Luke also record this incident it is only Mark who gives this particular detail.

Other omissions we merely note:

◾ John 6.47
AV: Verily, verily, I say unto you, He that believeth **on me** hath everlasting life.
NIV: I tell the truth, he who believes has everlasting life.

◾ Colossians 1.14
AV: In whom we have redemption **through his blood**, *even* the forgiveness of sins
NIV: In whom we have redemption, the forgiveness of sins.

🔲 1 Peter 1.22
AV: Seeing ye have purified your souls in obeying the truth **through the Spirit** unto unfeigned love of the brethren
NIV: Now that you have purified yourselves by obeying the truth so that you have a sincere love for your brothers

2. Addition

There are far fewer additions of material, perhaps a little over one hundred in the NIV. Some definitely affect the meaning. One example is:

🔲 1 Peter 2.2
AV: As newborn babes, desire the sincere milk of the word, that ye may grow thereby
NIV: Like newborn babies, crave pure spiritual milk, so that by it you may grow up **in your salvation**

God's people by grace through faith in Jesus Christ are now in a state of salvation. They **are** saved. Certainly sanctification is progressive and has degrees, but salvation in the sense of acquittal and reconciliation is complete when the sinner trusts in Christ and the Saviour's righteousness is imputed to him. This addition, along with other changes in the modern versions, tends to make salvation look like a process and fosters the Romish notion that the believer's works have merit. This is apparent at 1 Corinthians 1.18 where the AV has: 'For the preaching of the cross is to them that perish foolishness; but unto us which are **saved** it is the power of God'. The NIV has: 'For the message of the cross is foolishness to those who are perishing, but to us who are **being saved** it is the power of God'. Interestingly in this place there is no textual variant and so the difference in the rendering is to be explained purely as the preference of the translators.

3. Substitution

There are around five hundred substitutions in the NIV. Some are minor, involving the replacing of a word with the same word spelled differently, particularly personal names and place names. Others clearly affect the meaning. The following are some examples.

🔲 Mark 3.29
AV: But he that shall blaspheme against the Holy Ghost hath never forgiveness, but is in danger of eternal **damnation**
NIV: But whoever blasphemes against the Holy Spirit will never be forgiven; he is guilty of an eternal **sin**.

What, we may ask, is an eternal sin? We cannot say but we do know what eternal damnation is and so does everyone in his or her conscience before God.

⬛ Luke 6.48
AV: He is like a man which built an house, and digged deep, and laid the foundation on a rock: and when the flood arose, the stream beat vehemently upon that house, and could not shake it: **for it was founded upon a rock**.
NIV: He is like a man building a house, who dug down deep and laid the foundation on rock. When the flood came, the torrent struck that house but could not shake it, **because it was well built**.

The NIV here seems to teach that the believer's security does not depend on Christ alone but also on the quality of his own life, implying that works are effectual in our perseverance; clarity has been replaced by ambiguity.

⬛ Ephesians 5.9
AV: (For the fruit of the **Spirit** *is* in all goodness and righteousness and truth;)
NIV: (for the fruit of the **light** consists in all goodness, righteousness and truth)

The previous verse says that believers are light in the Lord and that they are to walk as children of light. We are to **be** in practice what we **are** by nature as those who have been born again and have the seed of regeneration in their hearts. We are to be holy in our **conduct** as we are in our **character**. Verse 9 is telling us how this holiness is possible and why it should be actual in our lives: the gracious working of the Holy Spirit produces a holy fruit in God's children.

These are **textual** changes. They alter the structure of Scripture. There is another type of change which does not affect the structure of Scripture but which is nevertheless important because it too affects the meaning of Scripture: **translational** change. This is where the Hebrew or Greek text underlying the modern versions is the same as that underlying the AV but the translators have rendered the words differently so that the meaning is affected.

4. Translation

Bible versions inevitably reflect the theological prejudices of their translators. There are certain key verses in the Old and New Testaments by which the various modern versions may be evaluated. Among these verses are:

📖 Isaiah 7.14

AV: Therefore the Lord himself shall give you a sign; Behold, a **virgin** shall conceive, and bear a son, and shall call his name Immanuel.

Revised Standard Version (RSV): Therefore the Lord himself will give you a sign. Behold, a **young woman** shall conceive and bear a son, and shall call his name Immanuel.

We know that whoever is born of ordinary generation inherits Adam's corrupt nature. It was necessary that the Son of God should be born by extraordinary generation to ensure the sinlessness of His human nature. Isaiah records the sign which will indicate the arrival of the Messiah in this world: a virgin shall be with child. It is perverse of the RSV to translate the Hebrew word *'almah* as 'young woman'. As J. Gresham Machen said: 'there is no place among the seven occurrences of 'almah in the Old Testament where the word is clearly used of a woman who was not a virgin'.[2]

📖 Daniel 3.25

AV: He answered and said, Lo, I see four men loose, walking in the midst of the fire, and they have no hurt; and the form of the fourth is like **the Son of God**.

New English Bible (NEB): He answered, 'Yet I see four men walking about in the fire free and unharmed; and the fourth looks like **a god.**'

There is every difference between 'the Son of God' and 'a god': the latter could refer to anybody who was highly esteemed by men. Surely it was only the presence of the true and living God in the Person of the Son that resulted in the miracle of the deliverance from the burning fiery furnace. This indirect testimony to the deity of Christ is lost.

📖 John 1.14

AV: And the Word was made flesh, and dwelt among us, (and we beheld his glory, the glory as of the **only begotten** of the Father,) full of grace and truth.

NIV: The Word became flesh and made his dwelling among us. We have seen his glory, the glory of the **One and Only**, who came from the Father, full of grace and truth.

In the AV the phrase 'only begotten' (or elsewhere 'only begotten Son') carries with it a distinct doctrinal significance. It means that Christ is the eternal and natural Son of the Father, of the same essence. The NIV abandons this precious phrase, replacing it with the ambiguous 'the One and Only' (John 1.14,18) or 'one and only Son' (John 3.16,18). Interestingly the Gideons, who in the UK customarily distribute the NIV, were given permission by the publishers to print and circulate a special edition of the NIV which retains the phrase 'only begotten' in the six places where the regular edition omits it.

◻ Acts 20.28

AV: Take heed therefore unto yourselves, and to all the flock, over the which the Holy Ghost hath made you overseers, to feed the church of God, which he hath purchased **with his own blood**.

Good News Bible (GNB, 1st edition): So keep watch over yourselves and over all the flock which the Holy Spirit has placed in your care. Be shepherds of the church of God, which he made his own **through the sacrificial death of his Son**.

Among the modern versions the Good News Bible in particular seems to have an aversion to any mention of blood (although this instance at least is corrected in the second edition). It views the term 'blood' as an emblem for death and systematically replaces the former with the latter in at least sixteen instances, some of which concern our Lord Jesus Christ. But though the two are related they are not identical. Scripture says, 'it *is* the **blood** *that* maketh an atonement for the soul' (Leviticus 17.11); 'without shedding of **blood** is no remission' (Hebrews 9.22). The emphasis on blood in Scripture reminds us of the nature of Christ's death: He made atonement for sin. This truth is repugnant to liberal theologians (and sadly to some modern 'evangelicals') because it emphasises the **holiness** of God when they want all the emphasis on the **love** of God. However, divine justice had to be satisfied by Christ and divine wrath pacified or else there could be no salvation for guilty sinners.

Even more is lost by this rendering. The AV indicates that the blood which purchased the church was the blood of a divine Person—God in our nature. The GNB and some other modern versions lose this indirect proof of the Godhead of Christ.

◻ Romans 8.28

AV: And we know that all things work together for good to them that love God, **to them who are the called according to** *his* **purpose**.

Living Bible (LB): And we know that all that happens to us is working for our good if we love God **and are fitting into his plans**.

This is a private interpretation, not a translation, and it is a wrong interpretation! It is a twisting of the text, doing down predestination and sovereign grace and exalting man's free will. This version was produced by one individual and he frequently intruded his false arminian views upon the text.

◻ Revelation 19.8

AV: And to her was granted that she should be arrayed in fine linen, clean and white: for the fine linen is the **righteousness** of saints.

New King James Version (NKJV): And to her it was granted to be arrayed in fine linen, clean and bright, for the fine linen is the **righteous acts** of the saints.

This rendering is acceptable according to the Greek but surely not correct according to the context which is the Marriage of Christ the Lamb of God and His Bride, the Church. On such an occasion we could never think of being covered spiritually with any robe but the perfect robe of Christ's own righteousness, imputed to us and received by faith. Are not all our 'righteousnesses' or 'righteous acts' 'as filthy rags' (Isaiah 64.6)?

A good translator will translate words in accordance with the overall teaching of the Bible or the **analogy of faith**. The doctrines of Scripture have been summarised and systematised in the historic creeds and confessions of the church. One of these confessions, the 17th-century *Westminster Confession of Faith*, itself explains how we should approach difficult passages of Scripture (Chap. I.ix): 'The infallible rule of interpretation of Scripture is the Scripture itself: and therefore, **when there is a question about the true and full sense of any Scripture (which is not manifold, but one), it must be searched and known by other places that speak more clearly**'.

We have seen what the devil does with the Word of God. We may now deal with the specific question, Which Version: Does it Really Matter? Again we will turn to Scripture to discover the principles which must guide us in identifying the true Word of God. We could say a lot about manuscripts, the findings of textual criticism and so on but in the end these things can never be decisive, especially for the man in the pew. How many Christians know Hebrew and Greek? How many who **do** know Hebrew and Greek have studied all or any of the Biblical manuscripts? There are nearly 5,500 catalogued Greek New Testament manuscripts in existence today! We believe that God has left us in His own Word the principles by which we are to know the true Word of God.

▉ Viewpoints on Versions

There are three general viewpoints which people have on the question of Bible versions.

First Viewpoint

Some people say that all versions of the Bible are really the same. They know that there are different versions of the Bible. They remember the old Authorised Version from their childhood. Now in their adulthood they are familiar with various modern versions. They can see that the style of the cover and the style of the English differ but in the end they can see no great difference between the versions. In their eyes all the versions deserve the title 'The Word of God', and any one may be safely used. It is simply a matter of one's own personal preference. Ask these people, Which Version: Does it Really Matter? and they would give a very simple reply: No! There are no changes of any importance. They have that attitude to religion which does not seem to see much harm in anything at all, anything that is apart from having clear and decided views in religion! Oh how oblivious they are to spiritual danger! They ignore the warning which Paul gave; 'For we are not as many, which corrupt the word of God' (2 Corinthians 2.17). We must beware of corrupters! There were those then and there are those now who corrupt the text and corrupt the teaching of the Bible.

We have to say that, apart from any other consideration, this position that all versions of the Bible are really the same fails already at the **practical** level. When we take a closer look at the contents of the different versions, we discover some **major** differences. For instance, we find that in most modern versions Mark's Gospel ends at chapter 16 verse 9 but in the Authorised Version it continues until verse 20. Similarly, in John's Gospel most modern versions omit twelve complete verses from 7.53–8.11 while the Authorised Version includes them. And there are individual verses missing from the modern versions, as we have already seen. What are we to do when we encounter these passages in our reading or in our preaching? Are we to make use of them or are we not? Are they the Word of God or are they not?

It is irrational to say in a post-modern sort of way that these opposites can **both** be true—yet this is often what is done. Many versions include these passages in the main text but inform the reader in footnotes that the 'most reliable manuscripts' do not contain them. What is the reader to think of this? It hardly reflects Peter's statement, 'We have also a **more sure** word of prophecy' (2 Peter 1.19). And how can one preach from passages such as the above if one has real doubts that they are the Word of God?

We should be clear that the textual differences between the Authorised Version and modern versions are not confined to just a few passages or a few words. Here are some figures to indicate the extent of the problem. (These or similar figures will be found in the many publications which cover this subject.) The figures relate to the text of the New Testament, where the problem largely occurs.

The Greek text underlying the New Testament in modern versions is approximately 2,500 words shorter than the Greek text underlying the New Testament in the Authorised Version. This is nearly 2% of the whole. It is the equivalent of removing 1 and 2 Peter from the Bible.

The total number of word differences (chiefly omissions, additions and substitutions) between these two texts is approximately 10,000 or nearly 7% of the whole.[3]

While many of these differences are minor, according to Everett W. Fowler[4] over 1,500 affect the meaning of the text and nearly 500 of these substantially affect the meaning. Biblical doctrine **is** at stake. So there are **theological** implications as well as practical problems if we take this viewpoint.

In the final analysis, this position—that all versions of the Bible are really the same even when they do not agree in many places on what the true, God-given, text is—cannot be held **logically**. It cannot be maintained alongside an orthodox, God-honouring doctrine of Scripture.

Second Viewpoint

Many people are of the view that the modern versions are definitely better than the old version, the Authorised Version. By modern versions we mean that sequence of versions which began with the Revised Version of 1881 and which has included the Revised Standard Version, the New English Bible, the Good News Bible, the New International Version and now the English Standard Version. This stream shows no sign of drying up yet; on the contrary the pace of publication has been increasing with the passage of time.

A consequence of this is that the 'shelf life' of modern versions seems to be decreasing. Which pulpits today use the Revised Standard Version—a version only fifty years old? Will the New International Version, only twenty-five years old, withstand the competition from the newly-arrived English Standard Version (the two versions are, of course, produced by rival publishers)? What effect does this rapid turnover of versions have upon respect for the Scriptures and memorisation of the Scriptures? These things alone should alarm anyone who reverences the Word of God and the God of the Word.

Many of those who use modern versions do so quite oblivious to the real departure they represent from the Authorised Version. Their thinking is, I want a Bible which speaks my language, or, I want a Bible which gets the gospel across to the young people of today. They believe that all that has really taken place in the modern versions is that the English has been made more up-to-date; the archaisms have been removed but the meaning retained.

The application of these two principles—we might call them **readability** and **relevancy**—has led to the casual, forgettable English which is the hallmark of so many of the modern versions. Let us consider **readability**. The idea is that the easier the Bible is to read the easier it will be to understand. This is simply not true. Listen to the apostle Paul: 'But the natural man receiveth not the things of the Spirit of God: for they are foolishness unto him: neither can he know *them*, because they are spiritually discerned' (1 Corinthians 2.14). A proper understanding of Scripture comes from the gracious work of the Holy Spirit which we term **illumination**. Significantly the definition of 'readable' given in one dictionary is: 'interesting without being of highest quality'.[5] Ought that ever to apply to the Bible? Surely we should aim for the very highest quality wherever the translation of the Word of God is concerned!

Let us consider **relevancy**. The idea is that the Bible must be accommodated to the present age. It must adopt the spirit of and speak in the language of the prevailing culture. It must be brought down to man's present level. But rather than the Bible being brought down to man's fallen level, fallen man must be lifted up to the Bible's level. This is the gracious work of the Holy Spirit which we know as **regeneration**.

Many of those who believe that modern versions are better than the AV believe that in the end it is the overall message of a verse which matters rather than its actual word content. So they are happy with paraphrases of the Bible, and versions which reproduce the **sense** of the original Scripture if not the exact words. Sometimes this approach to translation is termed 'dynamic equivalence'. That this was the approach of the NIV translators is clear from the NIV Preface: 'The first concern of the translators has been the accuracy of the translation and its fidelity to the thought of the biblical writers. They have weighed the significance of the lexical and grammatical details of the Hebrew, Aramaic and Greek texts. At the same time, they have striven for **more than a word-for-word translation**'.[6][emphasis mine]

It should be plain that a fundamental Biblical principle is compromised here: **inspiration**. All Scripture is given by inspiration of God and that inspiration is **verbal** in character. Look at Matthew 4.4: 'It is written, Man shall not live by bread alone, but by every **word that proceedeth out of the mouth of God**'. The individual words do matter and should be reproduced in any translation. Interpretation belongs to preachers, not translators.

But what is the **key** claim of those who advocate the superiority of the modern versions? Those who actually translate the modern versions, and especially those who have constructed and edited the Greek text which underlies the New Testament in these versions, do not believe that the modern versions merely modernise the

English. They believe that the true text of the New Testament was lost to the church for many centuries but it has now been recovered to supply the Greek text underlying the New Testament of the modern versions.

This was the thinking of the two men who promoted this idea in the 19th century—B. F. Westcott and F. J. A. Hort. They were behind the Revised Version of 1881 which we have already mentioned. They had an antipathy towards the Greek text known as the Received Text or Traditional Text which underlies the Authorised Version because of the theological clarity of this text.[7] Hort condemned the Received Text as 'vile' and 'villainous' and expressed his desire to rid the church of it.[8] But these two critics were faced with a stubborn fact: 85–90% of the available manuscript evidence for the New Testament text supported the Traditional Text—and still does. How could they explain this dominance? They invented the idea that there had been an official revision of the church's Greek text in the 4th century AD led by Lucian, Bishop of Antioch in Syria, whereby the Greek text popular there was imposed on the whole church. What Westcott and Hort viewed as the older, original form of the Greek text, often known as the Alexandrian Text after Alexandria in Egypt where it was popular, was thereby sidelined and entered into a long period of disuse, only to be brought by themselves into service again within the church 1,400 years later.

We should in fact be naturally disposed to view a text popular in Antioch with approval and a text popular in Alexandria with suspicion. Antioch was an early centre of apostolic labour. Paul and Barnabas preached there (Acts 11.25–26). In contrast Alexandria never had a visit from an apostle. It was a noted centre of heresy, particularly Gnosticism and Arianism—the belief that the Son of God is not of the same, one, underived essence with the Father but is the first creation of the Father through whom all else was created.

By this thinking another vital biblical principle is compromised: **preservation**. God has preserved His Word and that preservation is also **verbal** in character. Look again at Matthew 4.4: 'It is written, Man shall not live by bread alone, but by **every** word that proceedeth out of the mouth of God'. Every word matters. It is unthinkable then that God would allow some of the words of inspiration to be lost. But how and where has God preserved His Word?

It was the view of Westcott and Hort, one which is followed by most textual critics and many Christians today, that God has preserved His Word in certain key manuscripts of great antiquity—in fact in only **two** principal ones, known as Codex Vaticanus and Codex Sinaiticus. A 'thought for the day' by E. MacLelland in the *Choice Gleanings* Calendar for August 8, 2003, followed this line on preservation:

Miraculously preserved and beautifully displayed in the British Museum in London are many ancient manuscripts of the Scriptures. The Codex Sinaiticus, 4th Century, is carefully written on a hundred antelope skins. This great treasure was rescued from destruction in the nick of time. The Codex Alexandrinus, of the 5th Century, was also dramatically saved from fire, and is portrayed on hundreds of goatskin pages. God has miraculously preserved His precious Word. Do we treasure the Bible as we ought?[9]

But is this the fulfilment of God's promise to preserve His Word? We certainly have a promise of preservation in Scripture. 'For the LORD *is* good; his mercy *is* everlasting; and his truth *endureth* to all generations' (Psalm 100.5). 'The grass withereth, the flower fadeth: but the word of our God shall stand for ever' (Isaiah 40.8). 'Heaven and earth shall pass away, but my words shall not pass away' (Matthew 24.35). But how and where was this promise to be fulfilled? We note Isaiah 59.21: 'As for me, this *is* my covenant with them, saith the LORD; My spirit that *is* upon thee, and my words which I have put in thy mouth, shall not depart out of thy mouth, nor out of the mouth of thy seed, nor out of the mouth of thy seed's seed, saith the LORD, from henceforth and for ever'. God's Word is preserved, not in lying unused in the Pope's Library or in a wastepaper basket in a monastery on Mt. Sinai, but in **being used** by His people and being passed on from generation to generation down to the present day and until the end of time. Thus the compilers of the *Westminster Confession of Faith* in chapter I.viii could write that the Scriptures: 'being immediately inspired by God, and, by his singular care and providence, **kept pure in all ages**, are therefore authentical' [emphasis mine].

There is another Biblical principle which is compromised in the modern versions, one which is often overlooked: **repetition**. If a fact is to be settled beyond doubt then there is a Scriptural requirement which ought to be fulfilled: 'at the mouth of two witnesses, or at the mouth of three witnesses, shall the matter be established' (Deuteronomy 19.15). In Scripture the same teachings and even the same words are often found in more than one place. We turn once again to Matthew 4.4: '**It is written**, Man shall not live by bread alone, but by every word that proceedeth out of the mouth of God'. In His conflict with Satan Christ cited a text from Deuteronomy 8.3 and this was recorded by Matthew in his Gospel. But it was not only recorded by Matthew, it was also recorded by Luke (4.4). Significantly, in the NIV many of the relevant words are missing from Luke's account and the repetition is ruined.

Those who support modern versions will respond by saying, 'You are being unfair! The words are still there elsewhere in the Bible! Every doctrine is taught somewhere!' However, the point is that no man reads, teaches or preaches the whole text of the Bible at once! We study individual chapters and verses and consider their meaning—so changes at that level do matter greatly.

There is great wisdom in this principle of repetition. The truth is reinforced in our minds. Repetition helps us to retain the truth. But in the modern versions many of these repetitions are removed. An important example is in:

◾ Mark chapter 9:
AV: 43 And if thy hand offend thee, cut it off: it is better for thee to enter into life maimed, than having two hands to go into hell, into the fire that never shall be quenched:
44 Where their worm dieth not, and the fire is not quenched.
45 And if thy foot offend thee, cut it off: it is better for thee to enter halt into life, than having two feet to be cast into hell, into the fire that never shall be quenched:
46 Where their worm dieth not, and the fire is not quenched.
47 And if thine eye offend thee, pluck it out: it is better for thee to enter into the kingdom of God with one eye, than having two eyes to be cast into hell fire:
48 Where their worm dieth not, and the fire is not quenched.
49 For every one shall be salted with fire, and every sacrifice shall be salted with salt.
NIV: 43 "If your hand causes you to sin, cut it off. It is better for you to enter life maimed than with two hands to go into hell, where the fire never goes out.
[verse 44 is omitted from the text]
45 And if your foot causes you to sin, cut it off. It is better for you to enter life crippled than to have two feet and be thrown into hell.
[verse 46 is omitted from the text]
47 And if your eye causes you to sin, pluck it out. It is better for you to enter the kingdom of God with one eye than to have two eyes and be thrown into hell,
48 where 'their worm does not die, and the fire is not quenched.'
49 Everyone will be salted with fire."

The threefold repetition of identical words in this passage is surely designed to establish in our minds a solemn truth that we need to ponder but are prone to neglect: the eternal punishment of the impenitent. The NIV has severely weakened the force of this passage by removing two of the verses, referring to them only in footnotes.

As is quite well known, the word 'hell' is not to be found at all in the NIV Old Testament. It occurs thirty-two times in the AV Old Testament. Not all of these are references to the place of eternal punishment, but many are, including:

⬛ Psalm 9.17
AV: The wicked shall be turned into **hell**, *and* all the nations that forget God.
NIV: The wicked return to the **grave**, all the nations that forget God.

⬛ Proverbs 15.24
AV: The way of life *is* above to the wise, that he may depart from **hell** beneath.
NIV: The path of life leads upward for the wise to keep him from going down to the **grave**.

Third Viewpoint

Other people are of the view that the old version, the Authorised Version, is definitely better than the modern versions. They believe that in the AV, and in the Hebrew and Greek texts underlying that version, the true text of Scripture has been preserved for the church. These people are often scornfully dismissed as an ignorant minority. They are accused of inhibiting the gospel by their refusal to make the Word of God relevant to modern man. We may all agree that it would be a sin to hinder the progress of the gospel, but we should be careful not to denounce this viewpoint before we examine the reasons for holding it.

We could assess the competing versions according to various practical tests, such as we have indicated. We could also assess them according to various theological tests. We could ask both of the modern versions and their translators and the AV and its translators, What do you think of the doctrine of inspiration? or, What do you think of the doctrine of preservation? We believe that the answers given would be instructive. But there is a more fundamental question yet, the answer to which is vital in this whole debate.

⬛ The Christological Test

We wish to subject the competing versions to THE theological test. It is the **Christological test**. Jesus said to the Pharisees as He says to us all, 'What think ye of Christ?' (Matthew 22.42). This is the foundation which is of vital concern to us as sinners in need of salvation: the Person and Work of Christ. The Bible we use must be a safe guide here. It must not give an uncertain sound.

We look therefore at how the AV treats the Person and Work of Christ and what treatment the NIV as representative of the modern versions gives to the same. The type of textual change is indicated alongside the Scripture references.

The Person of Christ

While Christians are often in disagreement over certain doctrines and practices of their faith, a belief in the proper deity of Christ is agreed to be indispensable to being a Christian—something one simply must believe in order to be reckoned a child of God. The *Westminster Larger Catechism* Question 38 teaches us why it was so necessary that our Redeemer should be God:

> It was requisite that the Mediator should be God, that he might sustain and keep the human nature from sinking under the infinite wrath of God, and the power of death; give worth and efficacy to his sufferings, obedience, and intercession; and to satisfy God's justice, procure his favour, purchase a peculiar people, give his Spirit to them, conquer all their enemies, and bring them to everlasting salvation.

Let us remember though that we are to believe in the deity of Christ not firstly because a divine Mediator is necessary for our salvation but because this doctrine is revealed in the Bible and is therefore true and authoritative, whether we are personally deriving saving benefit from it or not.

It is this belief, along with that of the Trinity, that especially separates the true church of Christ from the range of deviant cults. One of the chief strategies in their proselytism is to attack these foundations. We have heard of Christians who have had the disturbing experience of being confronted by representatives of the so-called Jehovah's Witnesses who have bolstered their arguments, not only by reference to their own translation of the Bible, but also to Bible versions popular among today's evangelicals. This should not surprise us, for the 'New World Translation' of the Jehovah's Witnesses and the modern versions used by evangelicals are actually based upon the same Greek text.

The first generation of evangelicals which turned to new translations had been reared on the Authorised Version, which still shaped much of their belief and practice, but now we may meet professing Christians whose contact with the AV has been minimal or even non-existent. One sometimes wonders what view of Christ a man would come to if he were to be completely isolated from the church's historical Scripture text and commentaries based upon it and have only the modern text for his study?

We now look at some verses, mainly in the New Testament, which are important as far as the doctrine of the deity of Christ is concerned, making some brief comments on the differences in the renderings of the AV and the NIV.

1. Divine Names

⬛ 1 Timothy 3.16 (Substitution)

AV: And without controversy great is the mystery of godliness: **God** was manifest in the flesh, justified in the Spirit, seen of angels, preached unto the Gentiles, believed on in the world, received up into glory.

NIV: Beyond all question, the mystery of godliness is great: **He** appeared in a body, was vindicated by the Spirit, was seen by angels, was preached among the nations, was believed on in the world, was taken up in glory.

The name which most clearly establishes the deity of Christ is the name 'God' as applied to Him. By the removal of only two letters from the original Greek of this text one of the clearest proof-texts for Christ's deity is rendered useless. It could be said of every man who comes into the world that 'he appeared in a body'. C. H. Spurgeon commented on this text:

> Does it tell us that a man was manifest in the flesh? Assuredly that cannot be its teaching, for every man is manifest in the flesh, and there is no sense in making such a statement concerning any mere man, and then calling it a mystery. Was it an angel then? But what angel was ever manifest in the flesh? And if he were, would it be at all a mystery that he should be 'seen of angels'? Is it a wonder for an angel to see an angel? Can it be that the devil was manifest in the flesh? If so he has been 'received up into glory', which, let us hope, is not the case. Well, if it was neither a man, nor an angel, nor a devil, who was manifest in the flesh, surely he must have been God; and so if the word be not there, the sense must be there, or else nonsense.[10]

Moreover the footnote in the NIV which states 'some manuscripts *God*' is hardly honest when the great majority of Greek copies read 'God'—this reading also being attested by some of the earliest Church Fathers.

The real reason why this alteration is found in the modern text is understood from the history of the Revised Version of 1881. This project was originally sanctioned by the Church of England and intended as a limited revision of the Authorised Version. The final product however was based on the new Greek text of Westcott and Hort begun three decades earlier. The presence of Dr. G. Vance Smith, a Unitarian minister, on the revising committee provoked a row, with several thousand Anglican clergymen signing a protest, but Westcott and Hort defended his presence and he remained. The altered reading of 1 Timothy 3.16 was of course quite suitable to Dr. Smith, who wrote:

The old reading has been pronounced untenable by the Revisers, as it has long been known to be by all careful students of the New Testament... It is another example of the facility with which ancient copiers could introduce the word 'God' into their manuscripts—a reading which was the natural result of the growing tendency in early Christian times to look upon the humble Teacher as the Incarnate Word, and therefore as 'God manifested in the flesh'.[11]

Here is a mischievous idea. It is suggested that early Christians altered the text of the New Testament to make it 'more orthodox' than it originally was, and that by removing the word 'God' from this verse and other similar amendments the compilers of the Revised Version and subsequent versions have returned the text of the Bible to a purer state. The consequence of course is that one of the clearest statements of Christ's divinity is removed from the Bible, and that after multitudes of believers have for centuries derived instruction and encouragement from it. What sort of view of providential preservation is this?

By substituting the equivocal 'He' for the explicit 'God' the textual critics and the NIV translators have destroyed the value of this verse as a proof-text for the Incarnation, the essence of which, as seen in the *Westminster Confession of Faith* chapter VIII.ii, is: 'that two whole, perfect, and distinct natures, the Godhead and the manhood, were inseparably joined together in one person, without conversion, composition, or confusion'.

Other divine names applied to Christ are omitted in the modern versions. In the NIV New Testament the name 'Lord' is omitted from the text 35 times, the name 'Jesus' 38 times and the name 'Christ' 43 times.[12] Particularly serious is the way in which the name 'Lord' or 'Christ' has been separated from the name 'Jesus' at critical places:

◼ Luke 23.42
AV: And he said unto Jesus, **Lord**, remember me when thou comest into thy kingdom.
NIV: Then he said, 'Jesus, remember me when you come into your kingdom.'

◼ 2 Corinthians 4.10
AV: Always bearing about in the body the dying of the **Lord** Jesus, that the life also of Jesus might be made manifest in our body.
NIV: We always carry around in our body the death of Jesus, so that the life of Jesus may also be revealed in our body.

🔲 1 John 1.7
AV: But if we walk in the light, as he is in the light, we have fellowship one with another, and the blood of Jesus **Christ** his Son cleanseth us from all sin.
NIV: But if we walk in the light, as he is in the light, we have fellowship with one another, and the blood of Jesus, his Son, purifies us from all sin.

2. Divine Titles

🔲 Revelation 1.10–11 (Omission)
AV: I was in the Spirit on the Lord's day, and heard behind me a great voice, as of a trumpet, saying, **I am Alpha and Omega, the first and the last**: and, What thou seest, write in a book, and send *it* unto the seven churches which are in Asia…
NIV: On the Lord's Day I was in the Spirit, and I heard behind me a loud voice like a trumpet, which said: 'Write on a scroll what you see and send it to the seven churches…'

After hearing these words the apostle John turns to view the speaker who describes Himself by these titles, and John sees '*one* like unto the Son of man' (v.13)—in other words the glorified Jesus. Earlier, in verse 8, we find a Speaker taking to Himself the same titles, who is described as '…the Lord, which is, and which was, and which is to come, the Almighty'—this can only be God. Whether the Speaker in verse 8 is God the Father, Son or Spirit, it is established that the titles used are divine ones, and that Christ does not hesitate to take them to Himself: this proof of deity is lost in the NIV.

3. Divine Attributes

A. Eternity
🔲 Micah 5.2 (Translation)
AV: But thou, Beth-lehem Ephratah, *though* thou be little among the thousands of Judah, *yet* out of thee shall he come forth unto me *that is* to be ruler in Israel; whose **goings forth** *have been* from of old, from **everlasting**.
NIV: 'But you, Bethlehem Ephrathah, though you are small among the clans of Judah, out of you will come for me one who will be ruler over Israel, whose **origins** are from of old, from **ancient times**.'

Here is a vital verse from the Old Testament (partly quoted in the New Testament—Matthew 2.6; see also John 7.42). Apart from indicating that problems of text and translation are not wholly confined to the New Testament this prophetic verse is foundational to our understanding of the identity of Jesus of Nazareth: our perception of its contents will colour our view of the New Testament evidence concerning the Messiah. There is a world of difference between what is affirmed by these two versions here. The AV clearly teaches the eternal generation of the Son of God, Israel's King, by referring to His 'goings forth' and defining these as 'from everlasting'; the NIV by contrast gives the Son an origin or beginning, as though He were a son of God by creation, like the angels. According to the NIV God's Son is merely 'ancient' yet the NIV renders the same word as 'everlasting' when referring elsewhere to God's being and attributes.

B. Omnipresence
John 3.13 (Omission)
AV: And no man hath ascended up to heaven, but he that came down from heaven, *even* the Son of man **which is in heaven**.
NIV: 'No one has ever gone into heaven except the one who came from heaven—the Son of Man.'

Because of the remarkable union between the two natures in the Person of Christ He could be said to be present in heaven (according to His divine nature) while at the same time He was present on earth (according to His human nature): the NIV reading loses this precious testimony to a divine Mediator.

C. Goodness
Matthew 19.16–17 (Omission)
AV: And, behold, one came and said unto him, **Good** Master, what good thing shall I do, that I may have eternal life? And he said unto him, Why callest thou me good? *there is* none good but one, ***that is,* God**: but if thou wilt enter into life, keep the commandments.
NIV: Now a man came up to Jesus and asked, 'Teacher, what good thing must I do to get eternal life?' 'Why do you ask me about what is good?' Jesus replied. 'There is only One who is good. If you want to enter life, obey the commandments.'

In effect Christ was saying to the rich young ruler, 'Only call me good if you believe I am God'. Christ must be God or else He should not be called 'good', for only the Most High is **essentially, originally** good: the NIV has lost this indication of deity.

4. Divine Prerogatives

A. Worship
Matthew 8.2 (Translation)
AV: And, behold, there came a leper and **worshipped** him, saying, Lord, if thou wilt, thou canst make me clean.

NIV: A man with leprosy came and **knelt before** him and said, 'Lord, if you are willing, you can make me clean.'

The same alteration may be found in Matthew 9.18, 20.20 and Mark 5.6. In this instance the alteration is not due to change in the underlying Greek but to the choice of the translators. Is there not however a huge difference between these two renderings? One may properly kneel before an earthly monarch, but those coming to Christ were recognising the King of kings and paying Him the highest homage.

B. Judgment
📖 Romans 14.10,12 (Substitution)

AV: But why dost thou judge thy brother? or why dost thou set at nought thy brother? for we shall all stand before **the judgment seat of Christ**... So then every one of us shall give account of himself to God.

NIV: You, then, why do you judge your brother? Or why do you look down on your brother? For we will all stand before **God's judgment seat**... So then, each of us will give an account of himself to God.

In the text followed by the NIV and other modern versions verse 12 is simply a repetition of verse 10 which adds nothing to our understanding. In the Received Text we are taught clearly that to be judged by the Lord Jesus Christ is the equivalent of giving an account of our lives to **God**. This must be so because the judgment which declares our eternal destiny cannot be the right of any other but God.

The Work of Christ

Having looked at some passages which concern the doctrine of the Person of Christ, particularly His deity, we now look at passages relating to the Work of Christ, beginning with His entrance into the world.

1. Incarnation

📖 Luke 2.33 (Substitution)

AV: And **Joseph** and his mother marvelled at those things which were spoken of him.

NIV: The **child's father** and mother marvelled at what was said about him.

The sinlessness of Christ was secured by His extraordinary conception in the womb of the virgin Mary: there was no human father involved. It is true that Scripture does refer to Joseph as Christ's father, but only when recording the view of those who mistakenly termed him such, for example in Luke 2.48. On that occasion our Lord corrected Mary by His words in the next verse: 'wist ye not that I must be about my Father's business?' When Joseph and Mary are referred to as Jesus' 'parents' the idea is that together they were His legal parents, not necessarily His natural ones. The NIV breaks this rule and weakens the testimony to the most necessary doctrine of the Virgin Birth.

2. Commission

◢ John 9.4 (Substitution)
AV: **I** must work the works of him that sent me, while it is day: the night cometh, when no man can work.
NIV: 'As long as it is day, **we** must do the work of him who sent me. Night is coming, when no one can work.'

The Lord Jesus Christ was given by His Father, and willingly undertook, a unique commission: the office of Mediator between God and men. His miracles, performed in His own Name and by His own authority, attested that office. In contrast the apostles did signs and wonders only through Christ's Name (Acts 3.6–7; 4.10). Jesus often referred to His own special work (John 4.34; 5.19,36; 17.4). He intimated that what was about to happen to the blind man would be 'the works of God' (John 9.3); not only would the man's natural eyes be opened but also the eyes of his soul, for the Lord Jesus would send His Spirit into his heart. Christ is aware of His impending sufferings. During His earthly sojourn His works of healing and conversion show Him supremely to be 'the light of the world' (v. 5). The variant followed by the modern text, by placing Christ and the disciples on the same level, removes a reference to the Messianic Commission.

3. Crucifixion

◢ Matthew 20.22 (Omission)
AV: But Jesus answered and said, Ye know not what ye ask. Are ye able to drink of the cup that I shall drink of, **and to be baptized with the baptism that I am baptized with?** They say unto him, We are able.
NIV: 'You don't know what you are asking,' Jesus said to them. 'Can you drink the cup I am going to drink?' 'We can,' they answered.

What a graphic description the Lord gave of His approaching death: a baptism of blood! The blood that would dye His own garments would also 'sprinkle many nations' for their salvation (Isaiah 52.15), for 'without shedding of blood is no remission' of sins (Hebrews 9.22). It is a pity, to say the least, that this vivid indication of the atoning character of Christ's death is lost by tampering with the Greek text.

◾ Mark 15.28 (Omission)
AV: **And the scripture was fulfilled, which saith, And he was numbered with the transgressors.**
NIV: [omitted]

Countless prophecies were accomplished on the very day of Jesus' death, each one combining with the others to create in the believer's mind the solid conviction that Jesus is the Christ of God. The removal of this New Testament verse testifying to the fulfilment of a prediction regarding the Messiah in the Old Testament (Isaiah 53.12), and a similar change at Matthew 27.35, can only but weaken that conviction.

◾ 1 Peter 4.1 (Omission)
AV: Forasmuch then as Christ hath suffered **for us** in the flesh, arm yourselves likewise with the same mind: for he that hath suffered in the flesh hath ceased from sin
NIV: Therefore, since Christ suffered in his body, arm yourselves also with the same attitude, because he who has suffered in his body is done with sin.

A person reading or hearing this verse as given in the NIV would be excused if he failed to understand that Christ's sufferings were of a vicarious nature; a believer would lose that precious 'comfort of the scriptures' which helps his hope (Romans 15.4). A similar omission is found in 1 Corinthians 5.7.

4. Resurrection

◾ Mark 16.9–20 (Omission)
AV: **Now when *Jesus* was risen early the first *day* of the week...**
NIV: (The most reliable early manuscripts and other ancient witnesses do not have Mark 16.9–20.)

This section, which in fact has overwhelming manuscript evidence supporting it, contains details of Christ's resurrection appearances which are not found elsewhere in the Gospel narratives, particularly His rebuke of the disciples for their 'unbelief and hardness of heart' (v. 14) in rejecting the testimony of the believers who had seen Him alive. It is perhaps significant that one of these unbelieving disciples, Luke the beloved physician, later writes of 'many infallible proofs' by which Jesus showed

Himself alive during the forty days (Acts 1.3); the NIV and other modern versions prefer 'many convincing proofs'. The former has a reassuring objectivity about it whereas the latter is ultimately subjective; one person may not be convinced by what convinces another person.

◼ Ephesians 5.30 (Omission)
AV: For we are members of his body, **of his flesh, and of his bones.**
NIV: for we are members of his body.

What statement could emphasise more plainly that Jesus arose with the same body in which He died? The spiritual union of the church with her risen Head is as real and inseparable as the physical union of His literal body, which uniquely did not see corruption in the grave (Acts 2.25–32).

5. Ascension

◼ John 16.16 (Omission)
AV: A little while, and ye shall not see me: and again, a little while, and ye shall see me, **because I go to the Father.**
NIV: 'In a little while you will see me no more, and then after a little while you will see me.'

The Received Text, followed by the AV, has Christ speaking in a threefold way of His death, resurrection and ascension. Thus there is a clear, logical explanation of Christ's resurrection appearances: they form a brief episode prior to His ascension, for the encouragement and strengthening of the disciples (vv. 20–24). The NIV leaves the Lord in a kind of limbo, resurrected but not ascended, and yet as the disciples discuss their Master's words in the next verse they include the missing phrase (v. 17, NIV).

◼ Mark 16.19 (Omission)
AV: **…after the Lord had spoken unto them, he was received up into heaven, and sat on the right hand of God.**
NIV: (The most reliable early manuscripts and other ancient witnesses do not have Mark 16.9–20.)

While the NIV provides witness to the Ascension elsewhere, the denial of the authenticity of this passage spoils the church of the only verse in the Gospels that records what happened immediately following: Christ 'sat on the right hand of God' (v. 19).

6. Session

▣ Hebrews 7.21 (Omission)

AV: (For those priests were made without an oath; but this with an oath by him that said unto him, The Lord sware and will not repent, Thou *art* a priest for ever **after the order of Melchisedec**:)

NIV: but he became a priest with an oath when God said to him: 'The Lord has sworn and will not change his mind: "You are a priest for ever".'

We readily grant that this phrase comparing the priesthood of our Lord with that of the mysterious Old Testament figure is found earlier in the epistle and is included in the NIV text. This reference though is the only one in which the verse from Psalm 110 is quoted in full, with the prefatory oath, and applied in its entirety to Christ. Because of this we may indeed be sure that, like Melchisedec of whose death there is no record, Christ, living for ever, is making continual and effectual intercession for His people.

On a related theme, modern versions of the Bible make an assault on our Lord's teaching regarding prayer and fasting. The entire verse Matthew 17.21, 'Howbeit this kind goeth not out but by prayer and fasting', is missing from the text of the NIV, as is the phrase 'and fasting' from Mark 9.29. This is despite the fact that Jesus laid upon His people the duty of solemn fasting on occasions (Matthew 9.14–15). Could this sowing of the seed of doubt help to explain why the church has neglected this powerful spiritual weapon to her great disadvantage?

7. Revelation

▣ Matthew 25.13 (Omission)

AV: Watch therefore, for ye know neither the day nor the hour **wherein the Son of man cometh**.

NIV: 'Therefore keep watch, because you do not know the day or the hour.'

The return of Christ is described as His 'revelation' (1 Peter 1.13). This revelation is to occur at the consummation of the age, the exact time of which is kept hidden from men. The beautiful parable of the ten virgins, serving as wedding attendants, tells how the foolish five were caught unawares when the bridegroom finally came and so were shut out of the marriage celebration: they did not watch. How sad that the modern text ruins the application Jesus Himself makes at the conclusion of the parable, by removing the one phrase which indicates plainly that the story is teaching about Himself and His return and the imperative need which sinners have to be made ready for His return by the grace of the Holy Spirit. 'For he cometh to judge the earth: he shall judge the world with righteousness, and the people with his truth' (Psalm 96.13).

Conclusion

From the outset of his dealings with mankind the devil has sought to undermine our confidence in the Word of God, especially in those things which concern the Lord Jesus Christ. He has done this especially by promoting a corrupt text of Scripture as the true Word of God. When this text is subjected to the Christological test it is found to be seriously wanting concerning the Person and Work of Christ.

It would be quite wrong to say that modern versions such as the NIV bear no testimony to the truths we have been considering, as a systematic survey of the complete contents of these versions will show. Yet at the level of individual verses or passages there is a dangerous, cumulative undermining of important truths. The fact that these alterations go unnoticed by many who read modern versions or hear them read makes the matter all the more serious. Our stance concerning this vital subject should be clear: we should *shun* the modern versions.

In the Bible we read: 'If the foundations be destroyed, what can the righteous do?' (Psalm 11.3). Such an anxiety is a natural one for the believer. Just as a building which lacks a stable grounding is destined to come crashing down at length, so the true believer must have a sure basis for his faith: an inerrant Scripture.

In expounding Jeremiah 20.7 John Calvin wrote:

God indeed, could not be separated from his own truth; for nothing would be left to him, were he regarded as apart from his word. Hence a mere fiction is every idea which men form of God in their minds, when they neglect that mirror in which he has made himself known. Nay more, we ought to know that whatever power, majesty, and glory there is in God, so shines forth in his word, that **he does not appear as God, except his word remains safe and uncorrupted**.[13] [emphasis mine]

We believe that in our Authorised Version God's Word is to be found 'safe and uncorrupted'. Let us hold it fast, and the Saviour it faithfully presents to us.

David Blunt

References

1. Quotations here and throughout taken from the *Westminster Confession of Faith,* Edinburgh, Scotland: The Publication Committee of the Free Presbyterian Church of Scotland, 1967.

2. J. G. Machen, *The Virgin Birth of Christ* (Grand Rapids, MI, USA: Baker Book House, 1980), p. 288.

3. D. A. Waite, *Defending the King James Bible* (Collingswood, NJ, USA: The Bible for Today Press, 1992), pp. xii, 41-42.

4. Everett W. Fowler, *Evaluating Versions of the New Testament* (Watertown, WI, USA: Maranatha Baptist Press, 1981), p. 9.

5. *The Chambers Dictionary* (Edinburgh, Scotland: Chambers Harrap Publishers Ltd, 1999), p. 1374.

6. *The Holy Bible, New International Version* (London, England: Hodder & Stoughton, 1980), p. vi.

7. B. F. Westcott and F. J. A. Hort, *The New Testament in the Original Greek*, 2 vols. (London, England: Macmillan & Co., 1881), 1.115–116, 134–135.

8. Arthur F. Hort, *Life and Letters of Fenton J. A. Hort* (London, England: Macmillan & Co., 1896), 1.211.

9. *Choice Gleanings* (Port Colborne, ON, Canada: Gospel Folio Press, 2002), 8 August 2003.

10. C. H. Spurgeon, 'The Hexapla of Mystery', *Metropolitan Tabernacle Pulpit.* (CD-ROM, version 1.0. Albany, OR, USA: AGES Digital Library Sermons, 1997), p. 888.

11. Vance Smith in J. W. Burgon, *The Revision Revised* (Fort Worth, TX, USA: A. G. Hobbs Publications, 1983), p. 515.

12. Fowler, *op. cit.*, pp. 42-51.

13. John Calvin, *Commentaries*, vol. 3, *On the Book of the Prophet Jeremiah and the Lamentations* (Grand Rapids, MI, USA: Baker Book House, 1993), p. 27.

Bible versions referenced:

Good News Bible: *Good News Bible: Today's English Version,* 1st edition. London, England: The Bible Societies, 1976.

Living Bible: *The Living New Testament.* London, England: Hodder & Stoughton Ltd., 1972.

New English Bible: *The New English Bible.* Oxford, England: Oxford University Press, 1972.

New International Version: *The Holy Bible, New International Version.* London, England: Hodder & Stoughton, 1980.

New King James Version: *New King James Version.* Nashville, TN, USA: Thomas Nelson, Inc., 1982.

Revised Standard Version: *The Holy Bible, Revised Standard Version.* New York, NY, USA: Thomas Nelson & Sons, 1952.

The Rev. David Blunt is a minister of the Free Church of Scotland (Continuing) at North Uist and Grimsay.